Popular Music Theory

Grade One

by

Camilla Sheldon & Tony Skinner

A CIP record for this publication is available from the British Library.

ISBN: 1-898466-41-6

First edition © 2001 Registry Publications Ltd.

Published in Great Britain by

Registry House, Churchill Mews, Dennett Rd, Croydon, Surrey, CR0 3JH

Typesetting by

Take Note Publishing Limited, Lingfield, Surrey

Drawings of pop performers by Chris Challinor

Instrument photographs supplied by John Hornby Skewes Ltd.

Printed in Great Britain by MFP, Manchester.

Contents

4 Introduction and guide to music notation

clefs

notes

sharps

key signatures

stems

musical terms

8 Scales and keys

major and natural minor scales

pentatonic scales

scale notes

keys and key signatures

scale notation

scale degrees

13 Chords

chord symbols

notes in chords

chord notation

scale degrees

17 Rhythm notation

note and rest values

time signatures

eighth notes

grouping of notes and rests

21 Popular music

The Beatles

Elvis Presley

The Rolling Stones

Jimi Hendrix

26 Sample answers

27 Examination entry form

Introduction

This book covers all the new material you need to know to take the London College of Music Grade One examination in Popular Music Theory.

As well as helping you to pass the examination, the intention of this book is to introduce and explain the theory behind popular music and so help you improve your musicianship. You can benefit from working through the book whether or not you intend to take an examination. You will benefit most if you try out the information you learn in this book in a practical music-making setting, by relating the information to your instrument and by using it to create your own music.

This book is part of a series that offers a structured and progressive approach to understanding the theory of popular music and whilst it can be used for independent study, it is ideally intended as a supplement to group or individual tuition.

The book begins with a brief guide explaining the basics of music notation. It is essential that you study this section before proceeding to the rest of the book. The chapters of the book reflect the sections of the examination. Each chapter outlines the facts you need to know for the examination, together with the theory behind the facts. Each chapter is completed with some examples of the types of questions that will appear in the examination paper. The sample questions are intended to give a clear guide as to the types of questions that may be asked in the examination, however the list of questions is neither exclusive or exhaustive. Once you have worked through the questions at the end of each section you can check your answers by looking at the 'Sample Answers' in the back of the book.

As the requirements for each examination are cumulative, it is essential that you have a knowledge of the requirements for the previous grade. If you are not already familiar with this material, it is recommended that you also study the preceding *Preliminary Grade* book in this series.

Examinations are held twice a year and you can only enter for an examination by completing the stamped entry form at the back of each handbook.

We hope you enjoy working through this book and wish you success with the examination and all your musical endeavours.

Camilla Sheldon and Tony Skinner

Music notation is normally written on five lines that are known as a *staff* or *stave*. Each line, and each space between the lines, represents a different note. When you write music notation you have to be very careful that the noteheads are either dissected by a line, or are placed in the space between two lines.

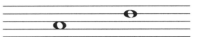

clefs

A *clef* is the symbol that tells you which notes are represented by the different lines and spaces.

 The *treble clef* (or *G clef*) tells you that the second line from the bottom is G.

 The *bass clef* (or *F clef*) tells you that the second line from the top is F.

All other notes progress in alphabetical order up and down each staff from these notes.

Temporary extra lines, known as leger lines, are used for any notes that are either too high or too low for a staff.

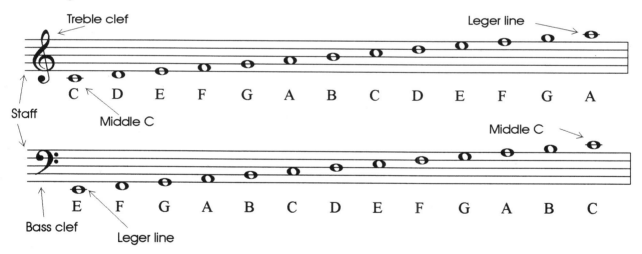

When writing a treble clef ensure that it curls around the G line.

When writing a bass clef ensure that you add a dot on either side of the F line.

notes

It is useful to have a few (mnemonic) phrases to help you remember the names of the notes on the clefs. Sometimes the sillier the phrases are, the easier they are to remember. Overleaf are a few we've made up with a 'wild animal' theme, but you might remember the notes even better if you make up your own unique phrases.

Lines in the treble clef

Eager Giraffes Bathe During February

Spaces in the treble clef

Fast Antelopes Can Escape

Lines in the bass clef

Grizzly Bears Don't Fear Anyone

Spaces in the bass clef

Angry Cheetahs Emerge Growling

There is a sharp note between most letter name notes. The only exceptions are between E and F, and between B and C. There is only a half step between these two sets of notes and so no sharps exist between them. If you look at the diagram of the piano keyboard below you will notice that there are no (sharp) notes between E and F, and between B and C.

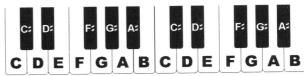

Therefore, the order of the notes in the musical alphabet progress like this:

writing sharps

When you write sharp notes on the staff, the # sign must be written to the left of the notehead. Depending on the note, the middle of the # sign should be either dissected by the same line as the notehead or placed in the same space as the notehead. When a sharp is written in front of a note it is called an *accidental*. Here is an example of F# written in both the treble and bass clefs.

sharps

Between most letter names there is a *whole step* (or *whole tone*). For example, the distance between the notes A and B is a whole step. However, you can also move just a *half step* (or *semitone*) up from any note by using signs known as *sharps* (#). For example, the note a half step above F is F sharp (F#). So F# is halfway between F and G.

key signatures

If a piece of music always uses an F# note rather than an F, instead of writing the sharp every time the note occurs, the music is given a *key signature.* The sharp sign is written across the F line at the start of every staff of music, between the clef and the time signature. This means that all the F notes are now played as F#.

stems

Half notes (minims), quarter notes (crotchets), and *eighth notes (quavers)* are written with a thin vertical line attached to the notehead. This is called a *stem*. It is important to write it in the correct direction. In simple melodies, stems go 'up on the right' if the note is below the middle line of the staff, and 'down on the left' if the note is above the middle line on the staff. The stems of notes on the middle line can go either way, depending upon the direction of the adjacent notes in the bar. Stems should be about the height of a staff in length.

musical terms

Sometimes there are two different names that can be used for the same musical elements. Also, the terminology that is widely used in N. America (and increasingly amongst pop, rock and jazz musicians in the U.K. and elsewhere) is different to that traditionally used in the U.K. and other parts of the world.

A summary of the main alternative terms is shown below. In the examination you can use either version.

whole note	=	semibreve
half note	=	minim
quarter note	=	crotchet
eighth note	=	quaver
whole step	=	whole tone
half step	=	semitone
staff	=	stave
measures	=	bars
keynote	=	tonic
$\frac{4}{4}$	=	**C**
treble clef	=	G clef
bass clef	=	F clef
flag	=	tail
leger line	=	ledger line

Use this space to write yourself some 'reminders' about the important points of music notation...

Section One – scales and keys

In this section of the exam you will be asked to write out and identify some of the following scales and keys signatures:

- C pentatonic major
- G pentatonic major
- A pentatonic minor
- E pentatonic minor

In addition, you should also have a knowledge of the scales set for the previous grade.

- C major
- G major
- A natural minor
- E natural minor

(If you are unsure about any of these requirements, please study the *Preliminary Grade* handbook).

So that the scales learnt in theory can be used effectively in a practical way, you should be able to do the following:

- Write out, and identify, the *letter names* that make up each scale.
- Write out, and identify, each scale in standard *music notation* (adding or identifying the key signature where appropriate). You can write your answers in either the treble clef or the bass clef.
- Write out, and identify, the *degrees* of each scale.

the theory

scales

A *scale* is a series of notes that are arranged in a specific order from the lowest note to the highest note. The note that is lowest in pitch is the first note of a scale. This note is also the one that sounds the strongest and is called the *keynote* (or *tonic*). The last note of the scale is the same as the first, but higher, and is known as the *octave*. Scales can be played ascending or descending, and notes from scales are used for writing melodies or for improvising.

major and natural minor

Major and natural minor scales are constructed using a combination of *whole steps* (also known as *whole tones*) and *half steps* (also known as *semitones*).

- A half step (H) is the distance from one note to the closest note above (or below) it, for example from F# to G.

- A whole step (W), for example from F to G, is double the distance of a half step; so a whole step is equivalent to two half steps.

`Major scales` are constructed using the pattern of whole and half steps shown below:

W W H W W W H

The C major scale, for example, is constructed in the following way:

■ C to the 2nd note (D) = whole step
■ D to the 3rd note (E) = whole step
■ E to the 4th note (F) = half step*
■ F to the 5th note (G) = whole step
■ G to the 6th note (A) = whole step
■ A to the 7th note (B) = whole step
■ B to the octave (C) = half step*

* Remember, that because there are no sharps between B and C, and between E and F, the gap within each of these pairs of notes is only a half step.

If you memorise this major scale 'step-pattern' (W W H W W W H) you will always be able to find out which notes make up any of the major scales. Simply start with the keynote and then use the step-pattern to find the other notes – making sure that, apart from the keynote and octave, each letter name is only used once.

The only major scales that are required for this grade are C major and G major; both of these have already been covered in the Preliminary Grade Handbook.

`Natural minor scales` are constructed using a different step-pattern to major scales. The step-pattern for natural minor scales is:

W H W W H W W

(Note that this is the same step-pattern as if the major scale had started on its sixth note).

The A natural minor scale, for example, is constructed as follows:

■ A to the 2nd note (B) = whole step
■ B to the 3rd note (C) = half step
■ C to the 4th note (D) = whole step
■ D to the 5th note (E) = whole step
■ E to the 6th note (F) = half step
■ F to the 7th note (G) = whole step
■ G to the octave (A) = whole step

If you memorise this pattern (W H W W H W W) you will always be able to find out which notes make up any of the natural minor scales. Simply start with the keynote and then use the step-pattern to find the other notes – making sure that, apart from the keynote and octave, each letter name is only used once.

The natural minor scales that are required for the Grade One exam are A and E natural minor. These have both been covered in the Preliminary Grade handbook.

pentatonics

Pentatonic scales are five-note scales. They are very useful for improvising as they contain fewer notes than the standard major or natural minor scales and so there is less chance of any of the notes clashing with the accompanying chords.

Pentatonic major scales are made up of five notes taken from the major scale with the same keynote. The five notes are the 1st, 2nd, 3rd, 5th and 6th. (When played or written as a scale the octave is also included). Notice that it is the 4th and 7th notes of the major scale that are omitted to create a pentatonic major scale.

Pentatonic minor scales are made up of five notes taken from the natural minor scale, with the same keynote. The five notes are the 1st, 3rd, 4th, 5th and 7th. (When played or written as a scale the octave is also included.) Notice that it is the 2nd and 6th notes of the natural minor scale that are omitted to create a pentatonic minor scale.

scale notes

Here are the names of the notes contained within the pentatonic major and pentatonic minor scales that are required for Grade One.

C pentatonic major:	C D E G A C
G pentatonic major:	G A B D E G
A pentatonic minor:	A C D E G A
E pentatonic minor:	E G A B D E

You should try and play these scales on your instrument so that you can hear the sound of them. Playing them will also help you memorise the notes that make up each scale. If you forget the names of the notes in these scales, you can work them out in the following way:

1. Use the 'step formula' to work out the notes of the major or natural minor scale with the same keynote.

2. Select the five notes that you need for the pentatonic scale you require.

For example, to find the notes in the C pentatonic major scale firstly work out the notes in the C major scale, then omit the 4th and 7th notes to convert it to the C pentatonic major scale.

Step formula	W W H W W W H
C major scale	C D E F G A B C
	1 2 3 4 5 6 7 8
C pentatonic major scale	1 2 3 5 6 8 C D E G A C

keys and key signatures

The *key* that a song is in determines the song's overall sound, known as its *tonality*. The key also determines which scale (and therefore which notes) will normally be used to make up the melody of that song. For example, if a tune is written in the key of G major it is likely to use notes from the G major or G pentatonic major scale. Because the keynote is the strongest note many tunes will begin and/or end with it.

A *key signature* tells you which key the music is written in. Key signatures are written immediately after the clef and are repeated on every new staff of music.

Here are the key signatures for the scales set for Grade One.

<u>G pentatonic major</u> and <u>E pentatonic minor</u>.

These two scales share the same key signature: one sharp, F#.

C pentatonic major and A pentatonic minor.

These two scales share the same key signature: no sharps or flats. So, in this instance, the key signature is effectively blank.

scale notation

Here are the four pentatonic scales required for Grade One, written out in both the treble clef and the bass clef:

C pentatonic major

G pentatonic major

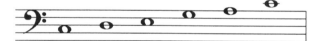

A pentatonic minor

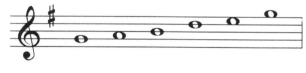

E pentatonic minor

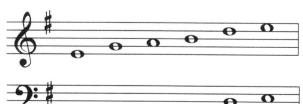

The notation for the C and G major and A and E natural minor scales is given in the *Preliminary Grade* Handbook.

scale degrees

In popular music, instead of using the letter names of the notes in a scale, musicians often use numbers. Each note of the scale is given a number, referring to its scale degree, starting with the keynote as '1'. For example, in the C major scale the notes are numbered as follows:

C D E F G A B C

1 2 3 4 5 6 7 8

So, rather than talking about the G note in the scale of C major, pop musicians might refer to it as the 5th degree of the scale.

As pentatonic scales are basically major or natural minor scales with some notes omitted, they do not have as many scale degrees as the full major or minor scales. This is illustrated in the tables below.

Scale / Degree	1	2	3	4	5	6	7	8
C major	C	D	E	F	G	A	B	C
C pentatonic major	C	D	E		G	A		C
G major	G	A	B	C	D	E	F#	G
G pentatonic major	G	A	B		D	E		G

Notice how the 4th and 7th degrees of the major scale are omitted in the pentatonic major scales.

Scale / Degree	1	2	3	4	5	6	7	8
A natural minor	A	B	C	D	E	F	G	A
A pentatonic minor	A		C	D	E		G	A
E natural minor	E	F#	G	A	B	C	D	E
E pentatonic minor	E		G	A	B		D	E

Notice how the 2nd and 6th degrees of the natural minor scale are omitted in the pentatonic minor scales.

the exam

Below are some examples of the types of questions that candidates may be asked in this section of the exam. If you can't answer a question, then carefully re-read the preceding chapter and the 'Guide To Music Notation' at the front of the book.

When answering questions that involve writing scales in notation, you can choose to write them in either the treble or bass clef. Either way, you need only write them ascending using whole notes (as shown here).

Q1. Which scale contains the notes C D E G A C?

A1. _____

Q2. Write the notes of the A pentatonic minor scale using letter names.

A2. _____

Q3. Write the notes of the G pentatonic major scale using letter names.

A3. _____

Q4. Write the key signature for G major in either the treble or bass clef.

A4. _____

Q5. Which scale is this?

A5. _____

Q6. Using the correct key signature, write one octave of the E pentatonic minor scale in either the treble or bass clef.

A6. _____

Q7. Which type of scale contains only the following scale degrees: 1 2 3 5 6 8?

A7. _____

Q8. On which degree of the C pentatonic major scale does the note E occur?

A8. _____

Section Two – chords

In this section of the exam you will be asked to write out and identify some of the following chords:

- C major 7th
- A minor 7th
- G major 7th
- E minor 7th

In addition, you should also have a knowledge of the triads set for the previous grade.

- C major
- A minor
- G major
- E minor

(If you are unsure about any of these requirements, please study the *Preliminary Grade* handbook).

So that the chords learnt in theory can be used effectively in a practical way, you should be able to do the following:

- Use *chord symbols* to identify the chords.

- Write out, and identify, the *letter names* and *scale degrees* that make up each chord.

- Write out, and identify, each chord in standard *music notation*. You can write your answers in either the treble clef or the bass clef.

the theory

chords

A *chord* is a collection of two or more notes that are sounded together. Chords can be used to accompany melodies or as backings for improvisation.

Major 7th and minor 7th chords consist of four different notes.

The 1st, 3rd, 5th and 7th notes of the major scale make up a major 7th chord.

C major scale		C major 7th
C	→	C
D		
E	→	E
F		
G	→	G
A		
B	→	B
C		

G major scale		G major 7th
G	→	G
A		
B	→	B
C		
D	→	D
E		
F#	→	F#
G		

The 1st, 3rd, 5th and 7th notes of the natural minor scale make up a minor 7th chord.

A natural minor scale		A minor 7th
A	→	A
B		
C	→	C
D		
E	→	E
F		
G	→	G
A		

E natural minor scale		E minor 7th
E	→	E
F#		
G	→	G
A		
B	→	B
C		
D	→	D
E		

chord symbols

The clearest symbol for a major 7th chord is the capital letter of the chord plus 'maj7': so the symbol for the C major 7th chord is Cmaj7 and the symbol for the G major 7th chord is Gmaj7. Major 7th chords can also be written like this: CMaj7 or Cma7. They are also sometimes seen written like this: CM7, C△ or C△7, but these symbols are not recommended as their meaning can be unclear.

The clearest symbol for a minor 7th chord is the capital letter of the chord plus lower case 'm' plus '7': so the symbol for the A minor 7th chord is Am7 and the symbol for the E minor 7th chord is Em7. Minor 7th chords can also be written like this: Ami7. They are also sometimes seen written like this: A-7.

C major 7th	=	Cmaj7
G major 7th	=	Gmaj7
A minor 7th	=	Am7
E minor 7th	=	Em7

notes in chords

Here are the names of the notes contained within the new chords added for Grade One. Notes within each chord are known as *chord tones*.

Cmaj7:	C	E	G	B
Gmaj7:	G	B	D	F#
Am7:	A	C	E	G
Em7:	E	G	B	D

You can work out which notes are contained within each chord by taking the relevant notes from the appropriate major or natural minor scale, with the same keynote, and then selecting the 1st, 3rd, 5th and 7th notes of this scale to form the chord. For example: to work out which notes are in the C major 7th chord, first work out the C major scale and then select the 1st, 3rd, 5th and 7th notes of this scale to form the chord; to work out which notes are in the A minor 7th chord, first work out the A natural minor scale and then select the 1st, 3rd, 5th and 7th notes of this scale to form the chord.

The 1st note of a chord (i.e. the note that gives the chord its name) is called the *root note*.

chord notation

Here are the four new Grade One chords in both the treble clef and the bass clef:

Cmaj7

Gmaj7

Am7

Em7

Notice that, in all major 7th and minor 7th chords, if the root note is on a line then the remaining notes of the chord occur on the adjacent lines above on the staff, whereas if the root note is in a space then the remaining notes occur in the adjacent spaces above.

scale degrees

In the same way that pop musicians often use numbers to talk about the notes in a scale, they sometimes use numbers to talk about the notes in a chord. Each note in the chord is given a number, which refers to the scale degree from which that note is taken.

For example, Cmaj7 is numbered as follows:

C E G B
1 3 5 7

In this example, rather than talking about the G note in the chord of Cmaj7, pop musicians might refer to it as the 5th note of the chord – because G is the 5th degree of the C major scale.

All major 7th and minor 7th chords are constructed using the 1st, 3rd 5th and 7th degrees of their related scales. This is illustrated in the tables below.

Scale / Degrees	1	2	3	4	5	6	7	8
C major scale	C	D	E	F	G	A	B	C
Cmaj7 chord	C		E		G		B	
G major scale	G	A	B	C	D	E	F#	G
Gmaj7 chord	G		B		D		F#	

Notice how the 2nd, 4th and 6th degrees of the major scale are omitted from the major 7th chords.

Scale / Degrees	1	2	3	4	5	6	7	8
A natural minor scale	A	B	C	D	E	F	G	A
Am7 chord	A		C		E		G	
E natural minor scale	E	F#	G	A	B	C	D	E
Em7 chord	E		G		B		D	

Notice how the 2nd, 4th and 6th degrees of the natural minor scale are omitted from the minor 7th chords.

Below are some examples of the types of questions that candidates may be asked in this section of the exam. If you can't answer a question, then carefully re-read the preceding chapter and the 'Guide to Music Notation' at the front of the book.

When answering questions that involve writing chords in notation, you can choose to write your answers in either the treble clef or the bass clef. You should place the notes of each chord vertically on top of one another, using whole notes (as shown in the example here). The notes of each chord should be written in *root position*, that means put the root note at the bottom, then write the third note, then the fifth and finally the seventh.

Q1. Which chord contains the notes G B D F#?

A1. _____

Q2. Write the notes of the Cmaj7 chord using letter names.

A2. _____

Q3. Write the notes of the Em7 chord using letter names.

A3. _____

Q4. Which chord is this?

A4. _____

Q5. Write out the Gmaj7 chord in either the treble or bass clef.

A5. _____

Q6. Is the note of E the 3rd or the 5th of the Am7 chord?

A6. _____

Q7. B is the 7th of which major 7th chord – Cmaj7 or Gmaj7?

A7. _____

Section Three – rhythm notation

In this section of the exam you will be asked to write out and identify some of the following note and rest values:

- whole notes (semibreves)
- half notes (minims)
- quarter notes (crotchets)
- eighth notes (quavers)

- whole rests (semibreve rests)
- half rests (minim rests)
- quarter rests (crotchet rests)
- eighth rests (quaver rests)

You will also be asked to use these notes and rests in $\frac{4}{4}$ time.

So that the rhythm notation learnt in theory can be used effectively in a practical way, you should be able to do the following:

- Write out, and identify, the symbols for the note and rest values listed above.
- Identify the values of different notes and rests.
- Explain how notes and rests of different values fit into bars (measures) of $\frac{4}{4}$ time.
- Group notes and rests correctly within $\frac{4}{4}$ time.
- Compose simple rhythms in $\frac{4}{4}$ time using the note and rest values listed.

the theory

note and rest values

Below are the names of the various note types required for this grade, the symbols for them and how many beats each type of note and rest lasts for in $\frac{4}{4}$ time.

name	note	rest	duration
eighth note (or quaver)			½ beat
quarter note (or crotchet)			1 beat
half note (or minim)			2 beats
whole note (or semibreve)			4 beats

Take note of the exact shape and position of the symbols used for rests.

A single eighth note (quaver) is written like this: ♪ or this: ♪

The tail or flag on an eighth note is always written to the right of the stem, regardless of whether the stem goes up or down.

When there are two eighth notes following one another, they are written with the stems joined by a beam. In 4/4 time, four eighth notes can be beamed together, as long as they are not beamed across the middle of the bar (i.e. on beats 3 and 4).

The diagram below shows the relative value of each type of note:

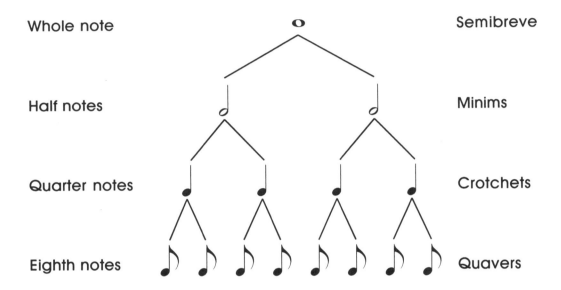

Whole note — Semibreve

Half notes — Minims

Quarter notes — Crotchets

Eighth notes — Quavers

time signatures

A time signature is written once at the beginning of a piece of music. It shows how many beats there are in each bar, and what type of note represents a beat. The top number shows the number of beats per bar, whilst the bottom number shows the type of note which represents a beat.

For example, this 4/4 time signature tells you that there are four quarter note (crotchet) beats in each bar.

The 4 at the top tells you that there are four beats in the bar.

The 4 at the bottom tells you that each beat is a quarter note.

(4/4 time can also be indicated by a 𝄴 sign).

When writing a time signature, the tip of the top number should touch the top line of the staff, and the base of the bottom number should touch the bottom line of the staff. The time signature should always be written after the clef and the key signature. The time signature should only be written in the first bar of a piece of music – it does not need to be repeated on each staff of music.

eighth notes

An eighth note lasts for half the duration of a quarter note. It can be played when the beat starts, and halfway through the beat.

Eighth notes played when the beat starts ('on the beat') are written:

Eighth notes begun halfway through the beat ('off the beat') are written:

grouping of notes & rests

In $\frac{4}{4}$ time each bar must add up to the equivalent of four quarter note beats, whatever the combination of note and rest values.

There are certain rules about how combinations of these notes can be written. These rules exist in music notation so that all four beats of the bar can be clearly identified, and consequently the written music is easier to read.

At this level you should be aware of the following rules in $\frac{4}{4}$ time:

Rule 1

Notes shorter than a quarter note are grouped together to form a beat.

For example, you can beam together two eighth notes that start on a beat, but you should not beam together two eighth notes that belong to two different beats.

This is correct.

This is incorrect.

There is an exception to this rule:

1) You can beam together four eighth notes that are in the first half of the bar (beats 1 and 2) or in the second half of the bar (beats 3 and 4). However, you should not beam together eighth notes in the middle of the bar (beats 2 and 3), instead you should use two pairs of beamed eighth notes.

This is correct.

This is incorrect.

Rule 2

Unless there is a whole bar rest, each quarter note beat should have a separate rest.

There is an exception to this rule:

You can write a half rest in the first half of the bar (beats 1 and 2) or in the second half of the bar (beats 3 and 4). However, you should not write a half rest in the middle of the bar (beats 2 and 3), instead you should use two quarter rests.

This is correct.

This is incorrect.

Below are some examples of the types of questions that candidates may be asked in this section of the exam. If you can't answer a question, then carefully re-read the preceding chapter and the 'Guide To Music Notation' at the front of the book.

Q1. What type of note is this?

A1. _____

Q2. What type of note is this?

A2. _____

Q3. Write the symbol for a quarter note (crotchet) at a pitch of your choice. Use either the treble or bass clef.

A3. _____

Q4. Write out the symbol for an eighth (quaver) rest. Use either the treble or bass clef.

A4. _____

Q5. What type of rest is this?

A5. _____

Q6. How many eighth notes (quavers) are there in a half note (minim)?

A6. _____

Q7. How many quarter notes (crotchets) are there in a whole note (semibreve)?

A7. _____

Q8. Complete the following bars by inserting the appropriate rest or rests in the spaces marked *.

A8.

Q9. At a pitch of your choice, write a two bar rhythm in $\frac{4}{4}$ time using quarter notes (crotchets) and eighth notes (quavers) and their equivalent rests. Use either the treble or bass clef.

A9. _____

Section Four – popular music

So that you begin to gain a general knowledge of the groups, vocalists and instrumentalists who have had the greatest influence on the development of popular music, in this section of the exam you will be asked questions about the following artists and groups:

- The Beatles
- Elvis Presley
- The Rolling Stones
- Jimi Hendrix

You may be asked to name:

- Some of their hit recordings.
- Some members of the group (where appropriate).
- The instruments played by instrumentalists.
- The period during which they performed or recorded.

Below is a short profile giving all the information you need about each artist and group for the Grade One exam. We recommend, that as well as reading their profiles, you also listen to some recordings by them so that you can begin to develop an idea of their musical styles.

The Beatles

This British group is widely recognised as being the most influential pop group of all time. The members of the group were:

- John Lennon
- Paul McCartney
- George Harrison
- Ringo Starr

The group's lead singers and songwriters were John Lennon and Paul McCartney (although sometimes George Harrison and Ringo Starr both sang and wrote songs). Their ability to write their own songs has inspired many other pop musicians to do the same, rather than relying upon professional songwriters.

Harrison, Lennon, McCartney and Starr of the Beatles

All members of the group played a variety of instruments, but their main instruments are listed below:

- John Lennon – guitar
- Paul McCartney – bass guitar and piano;
- George Harrison – guitar
- Ringo Starr – drums.

The group began in 1960 and, after various line-up changes, had their first hit record, *Love Me Do*, in 1962. They achieved enormous popularity during the 1960s and had many hit records before they split up in 1970. They recorded a range of musical styles including pop, rock, ballads and psychedelia. *The Beatles* remain one of the best selling groups ever.

Here are some of their most famous singles:

- *She Loves You*
- *A Hard Day's Night*
- *Get Back*
- *Hey Jude*
- *All You Need Is Love*
- *Strawberry Fields Forever*

Elvis Presley

American-born Elvis Presley had his first major hit single in 1956, with *Heartbreak Hotel*. Elvis went on to become the most successful and inspirational vocalist

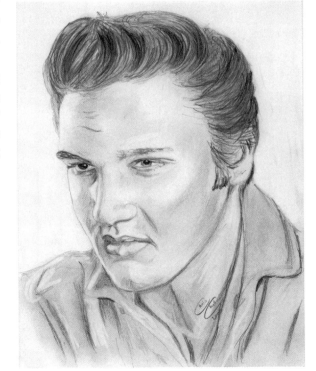

and performer in the history of popular music. Although he didn't write many songs himself, his career spanned three decades from the fifties to the seventies. He achieved world-wide popularity during his lifetime, and even since his death in 1977 he remains idolised by fans all over the world. He had success with a wide range of musical styles, from earthy rock 'n' roll to orchestral ballads.

Some of his most famous singles are:

- *Heartbreak Hotel*
- *Blue Suede Shoes*
- *Love Me Tender*
- *Hound Dog*
- *Jailhouse Rock*
- *Suspicious Minds*

The Rolling Stones

The British rock group, *The Rolling Stones,* has enjoyed the longest lasting success of any group in the history of popular music.

The group was formed in 1962, achieved its first UK chart success in 1963, and (at the time of writing) is still hugely popular both as a live act and in terms of recording sales.

Whilst there have been some line-up changes during the group's long career, the original members are:

- Mick Jagger – vocals

- Keith Richards – guitar

- Charlie Watts – drums

- Bill Wyman – bass

- Brian Jones – guitar

Guitarist Mick Taylor replaced Brian Jones, after Jones died in 1969. Ron Wood replaced Mick Taylor after he left in 1974. In 1995 bassist Bill Wyman left.

Wyman, Watts, Wood, Jagger and Richards of the Rolling

Although the Rolling Stones' earliest records were cover versions of other peoples' songs, most of the group's records since have been written by Mick Jagger and Keith Richards.

Here are some of the group's most famous singles:

- *(I Can't Get No) Satisfaction*

- *Paint It Black*

- *Get Off Of My Cloud*

- *Honky Tonk Woman*

- *Jumpin' Jack Flash*

- *Start Me Up*

Jimi Hendrix

American-born Jimi Hendrix is one of rock history's most respected and influential guitarists. Although he played in the backing groups of well-known artists, such as Little Richard and James Brown during the early 1960s, his solo career only began in 1966 and lasted for just four years until his death in 1970. During this time however, he revolutionised electric guitar playing as well as having several hit records.

The majority of his hits were with his band the *Jimi Hendrix Experience*, the members of which were:

- Jimi Hendrix – guitar and vocals
- Noel Redding – bass
- Mitch Mitchell – drums

These are some of his most famous recordings:

- *Hey Joe*
- *Purple Haze*
- *Little Wing*
- *All Along The Watchtower*
- *Red House*
- *The Wind Cries Mary*

the exam

Below are some examples of the types of questions that candidates may be asked in this section of the exam. If you can't answer a question, then carefully re-read the preceding chapter.

Q1. Name the drummer of The Beatles.

_____

Q2. Name one of Elvis Presley's hit records.

_____

Q3. Name the vocalist of The Rolling Stones.

_____

Q4. In which decade did The Jimi Hendrix Experience perform and record?

_____

Section Five – sample answers

Section One – scales and keys   *[Max. 40 marks]*

A1. C pentatonic major

A2. A C D E G A

A3. G A B D E G

A4.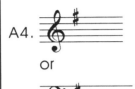

or

A5. G major

A6.

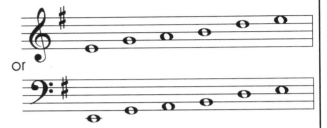

or

A7. Pentatonic major

A8. 3rd

Section Two – chords   *[Max. 35 marks]*

A1. Gmaj7

A2. C E G B

A3. E G B D

A4. Am7

A5.

A6. 5th

A7. Cmaj7

Section Three – rhythm notation   *[Max. 13 marks]*

A1. Eighth note (or quaver)

A2. Half note (or minim)

A3.

A4.

A5. Half rest (or minim rest)

A6. Four

A7. Four

A8.

A9.

Section Four – knowledge of popular music   *[Max. 12 marks]*

A1. Ringo Starr

A2. Blue Suede Shoes (a range of other answers would be acceptable)

A3. Mick Jagger

A4. The 1960s

Examination Entry Form for LCM
Popular Music Theory examination.

GRADE ONE ONLY

PLEASE COMPLETE CLEARLY USING BLOCK CAPITAL LETTERS

SESSION (Summer/Winter): _____ YEAR: _____

Preferred Examination Centre (if known): _____
If left blank, you will be examined at the nearest examination centre to your home address.

Candidate Details:

Candidate Name (as to appear on certificate):

_____

Address: _____

_____

_____ Postcode: _____

Tel. No. (day): _____ (evening): _____

Teacher Details:

Teacher Name (as to appear on certificate): _____

Registry Tutor Code (if applicable): _____

Address: _____

_____ Postcode: _____

Tel. No. (day): _____ (evening): _____

IMPORTANT NOTES

- It is the candidate's responsibility to have knowledge of, and comply with, the current syllabus requirements. Where candidates are entered for examinations by teachers, the teacher must take responsibility that candidates are entered in accordance with the current syllabus requirements. In particular, from 2005 it is important to check that the contents of this book match the syllabus that is valid at the time of entry.

- For candidates with special needs, a letter giving details should be attached.

- Theory dates are the same worldwide and are fixed annually by LCM. Details of entry deadlines and examination dates are obtainable from the Examinations Registry.

- Submission of this entry is an undertaking to abide by the current regulations as listed in the current syllabus and any subsequent regulations updates published by the LCM / Examinations Registry.

- UK entries should be sent to The Examinations Registry, Registry House, Churchill Mews, Dennett Rd, Croydon, Surrey CR0 3JH

- Overseas entrants should contact the LCM / Examinations Registry for details of their international representatives.

Examination Fee   £ _____

Late Entry Fee (if applicable)   £ _____

Total amount submitted: £ _____

Cheques or postal orders should be made payable to The Examinations Registry.
Entries cannot be made by credit card.

A current list of fees is available from the Examinations Registry.

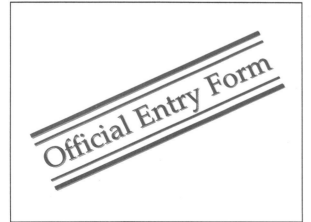

This examination entry form should be sent to our
NEW ADDRESS:

The Examinations Registry
Registry Mews
11 to 13 Wilton Road
Bexhill, E. Sussex, TN40 1HY

Tel: 01424 22 22 22
Email: mail@ExamRegistry.com